Power Words for

Prosperous Living!

by John Wolcott Adams

Published by Golden Key Publications
P.O. Box 1463
Mesa, AZ 85211-1463 USA

Power Words for
Prosperous Living!

ISBN: 0-9602166-1-8

First Printing, May 1984
Second Printing, October 1988

Printed in the UNITED STATE OF AMERICA
by Arcata Graphics, Kingsport, Tennessee

Other books by the Same Author

BE What You Are: LOVE
Thirty Days To A Better Life
Positively Alive!

Tapes by the Author

Money is Wonderful!
Two-Cassette Album

Prosperous Living Power!
The 200 affirmations from this book

How To Demonstrate Abundant Prosperity

This book is lovingly dedicated to the memory of my mother, Alice D. Adams, who loved and lived by the principles set forth in this book, and who had a very positive influence upon my life.

In loving appreciation . . .

I am especially grateful for Carol Thatcher who so lovingly set the type for this book, and to all of my teachers through the years who have helped me learn and live the positive, affirmative way of life. My special thanks to Richard Montague who introduced me to affirmations and to the late Dr. Adolph N. Meyer who first inspired me with the Truth teaching. I love you all!

John Wolcott Adams

Contents

Introduction . . . .

What this book will do for you . . . A personal message from the author.

This book will give you "Golden Keys" for unlocking from within you, your vast potential for happy, healthy, successful and prosperous living. In it you will find practical things to do that are of immense value to you. It will teach you the affirmative way of life that thousands of others are using every day to make their lives more positive and satisfying.

As you use this book as it is intended, you will build true prosperity consciousness that must express in your life as prosperous living. Do not under-estimate the effectiveness of using ***Power Words for Prosperous Living***. What you declare is what you usually get. By making positive, prosperous declarations, you tap the infinite spiritual resources within you and they pour into your life as happy, prosperous blessings.

Some people waste their precious thought and word power in thinking and speaking negatively; in degrading themselves, and in giving energy to lack and limitation. This is unfortunate, especially when they could just as well use the same thought and word power to intelligently bless themselves and live happy lives.

Fortunately, though, many more people are learning to use the affirmative process to build positive belief systems through speaking prospering words and focusing their attention upon right ideas. They have learned to accept themselves as worthwhile, and therefore, deserving children of God who *should* experience good health, happiness, success and prosperity—in abundance!

God did not put you here to suffer; to do without; to degrade yourself or others, and never to live in lack and limitation. His will for you is to live and enjoy the good life now. He has given you all you need to do that, and keeps on giving to you. This book will help you become a more open channel through which He may pour His infinite riches into your life. It will help open the Universal floodgates of prosperity so that money and all the other good things of life will be yours.

By applying the teaching of this book, and especially when you use daily, the prosperity affirmations, you will have many wonderful experiences and learn how to "Golden Key" your goals and have them manifest in your life so much more easily.

This was true with a successful executive with a large insurance company in New York City. She wrote:

"I am happy to report that everything worked out perfectly as we all 'Golden Keyed' this divine change in our lives. That is how my perfect place of residence came to me which is the affirmation I used and asked you to pray with me. Things worked out even better than my highest expectations.

"I have been affirming, 'THE UNIVERSAL FLOODGATES OF PROSPERITY BURST OPEN WIDE, POURING LOTS OF MONEY INTO MY LIFE NOW!' Using this affirmation has really worked for me. Thank you for your help."

You, too, will learn to "Golden Key" your goals and any situation that comes to you. Challenges will no longer be things that would otherwise put you down, but opportunities to make your positive declarations and rise victoriously onto a higher plane of successful activity.

In this book, you will find "just the affirmation you need" for some specific problem, challenge, or desire. As you speak prosperity affirmations daily, you will realize why they are called "*Power Words* for Prosperous Living!" And, you will see some wonderful changes take place in your life. This book will become a good friend, and a valuable asset to you and your loved ones.

May it truly bless you with all the good things of life and be a real inspiration to you to live the prosperous life!

John Wolcott Adams
P.O. Box 1463
Mesa, AZ 85201

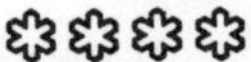

When the file cabinets of the mind are filled with thoughts of strength, health, beauty, honesty, efficiency, economy, and prosperity, there God-designed energy constantly attunes every fiber of your being to respond to and express these positive, perfect qualities in every department of your life. You cannot help manifesting the good that you think!

—Clifton J. Noble

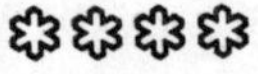

Your Spoken Word is Power!

You have within you the power to make your life what you desire it to be. Your spoken word is not only powerful to make changes in your life, it is the power through which definite changes come about. Regardless of outside influences, you shape your life through your thoughts and words. You do this whether or not you are aware of it.

When you know the power of words, especially your spoken words, you will put a guard at your lips and be very wise in what words pass through, just as you will do the same with your ears in that you will allow only that which is uplifting, positive and life-enriching to enter and find lodging in your thinking process.

You will focus your eyes upon that which

teaches you the truth that makes you free; that lifts you on high and inspires you to happy, sensible and prosperous living.

Words mold and shape your life.

Words can make your life miserable or marvelous, it is up to you. Just as what you think makes you what you are, words mold and shape your life because words are the expressions of thought; ideas held in mind. Negative words result in negative, unhappy experiences—positive words result in positive, happy and prospering experiences.

Jesus Christ, the Great Prosperity Teacher, pointed out the power of words when He said, "By your words you shall be condemned," and "death and life are in the power of the tongue."

You have the power to change undesirable financial circumstances through the power of your word. If you have only a few dollars, don't waste time in lack-thinking. Get busy sincerely blessing the money as you hold it in your hands, in the understanding faith that your blessing will multiply it and bring you more. Thankfully give it forth knowing it is returning to you as a harvest of multiplied money. This often works miracles! It is much better than fearfully hanging on to it, afraid there will be none to take its place. Blessing and releasing money is magnetic. Lovingly release it knowing more is coming now.

Charles Fillmore, co-founder of Unity School of Christianity, pointed out that spiritual thoughts are infinite in their potentiality, each one being measured by the life, intelligence, and substance with which it is expressed. The thought is brought forth into expression and activity by the word. Every word is a thought in activity, and when spoken it goes out as a vibratory force that is registered in the all-providing substance.

Think before you speak.

Did you ever think that your word is charged with infinite spiritual life force? It is!

If this thinking is new to you, be sure to give sufficient thought to the ideas shared with you here. Understanding will bring the assurance that this teaching is practical as well as dynamic. To those who are familiar with the power of the mind and of words, it is nothing new. You know it is very important to watch your words; to speak in an upward, positive way so that what you say comes back to you in pleasant and satisfying results.

You are mindful to speak in accord with what you desire to accomplish and never in a way that is contrary to the upward, progressive intent of the

Universe, and what you are giving your energy toward achieving.

It means, simply, you THINK BEFORE YOU SPEAK drawing from within you, infinite love and wisdom that express in wise and constructive words. Words are thoughts expressed.

You are held accountable for your slightest word. This doesn't mean that a capricious Being is going to strike you down for uttering a wrong word, or keep track of what you say, for later punishment. Neither is a person going to necessarily react negatively toward you for speaking unwisely, but that you are dealing with the law of cause and effect. (Of course, if you say something derogatory to someone, you may reap an immediate —and sometimes violent—reaction, just as when saying something kind usually reaps a kind response.)

What you declare makes a difference

In speaking words, you are literally moving substance, making a definite difference some where in some way. Most of all, you are making a definite, although seemingly imperceptible, difference within yourself and upon the conditions of your life. That is why there is specific benefit to you when you consciously and deliberately make prosperous declarations by using the affirmations in this book.

To affirm something is to decree. You are decreeing that something is so. Doing this with understanding faith is sure to result in satisfying experiences. It is so much better to make definite positive declarations than to ignorantly decree (affirm) negative things.

Substance is always within and around you, responding to your thought and word. Charles Fillmore wrote, "The spiritual substance from which comes all visible wealth is never depleted. It is right with you all the time and responds to your faith in it and your demands upon it. It is not affected by our ignorant talk of hard times, though we are affected because thoughts and words govern our demonstration." *("Prosperity"—Unity Books)*

If you talk in a negative downward manner, substance responds to your words and your finances tend to decrease. When you talk in a positive, upward manner, especially in decreeing prosperity affirmations, substance responds to your words and your finances improve. It is, therefore, wise and beneficial to always speak words that are upward and are the embodiment of positive, prospering ideas and energy.

Cease Idle Chatter

As people learn of the power of speaking affirmations they realize the wisdom and efficacy of this dynamic spiritual process, and they experience the happy results in their lives. Understandably, they cease from idle chatter about non-essential things.

People who spend minutes and hours in conversation that is often negative, demeaning and useless, are ignorant of the power of their words. If they would cease that non-productive activity, stop wasting their good time and energy, and engage in more intelligent conversation, they would be amazed at the positive change in their lives. If they would then spend just fifteen minutes in daily speaking prosperity affirmations, they'd experience even greater changes in their lives. *It would seem like a miracle!*

Of course, it is much better to speak affirmations for more than fifteen minutes daily, depending upon your need and your desire to prosper. However, do not over-effort in speaking prosperity affirmations. A few very powerful declarations will do more than glibly speaking many.

An important thing to remember: In between the times of making your positive declarations, don't give even one moment to negative or non-constructive thought or conversation. To do so, cancels the good you do through speaking prosperity affirmations.

Watch your words!

Listen to what you are saying. Make your words conform to that which is positive and prosperity-producing. Declare only that which you want to see demonstrated in your life. Right words will make your life more enjoyable, happier, more successful and prosperous.

Right words prosper her!

A lady who was divorced and un-employed, and with two small children, sought the help of a spiritual counselor. It was evident, she had spent much of her life thinking and speaking in a negative, self-demeaning way. Her unhappiness compounded as she went from one negative experience to another. Nothing seemed to go right. How could it?

The counselor helped her to listen to herself; to *hear* the words she spoke, and to understand how, through her thoughts and words, she had the power to transform her life.

A little dis-believing, at first, she was wise enough to know she must do something so that she and her children's lives would be happier and she would have money to pay her bills and for food, rent and clothes. She was ready to do whatever was needed to affect a change for the better.

She was instructed to watch her thoughts and words, and to use prosperity affirmations. She began immediately declaring, "THROUGH THE POWER OF MY THOUGHT AND WORDS, POSITIVE CHANGES ARE HAPPENING IN ME AND IN MY LIFE NOW." She also decreed, "I AM WISE, LOVING, AND HAPPY, AND GOD IN ME IS PROSPERING ME ABUNDANTLY NOW!"

The next day she called to say she had received some money quite unexpectedly, and a few days later, she reported she had found a job that, although not providing for luxuries, would give her enough money for herself and her children.

Continuing to make her prosperity declarations, she later reported the company liked her so much they had given her a new position with a substantial raise in pay.

In addition to speaking affirmations, she began to tithe, giving back to God, at least ten percent of her gross income, in gratitude for all that God was giving her. Now, she is prospering in an even larger way—enjoying the prosperous life. She said it was amazing how the children's school work improved and the family environment was happier as her children joined with her in speaking prosperity affirmations.

Start early!

It is, of course, wise to teach children the affirmative way of life through the speaking of affirmations. When they are taught early, to use affirmations, it stays with them throughout their lives creating for them, much more happiness, good health, success and prosperity.

People who are wise; who are clear in their desire for true, overflowing prosperity, and who have learned to use prospering words, spend at least a few minutes in daily speaking *Power Words for Prosperous Living*. They know, prosperity affirmations build prosperity consciousness which in turn expresses in prosperous conditions.

Prosperous thinking precedes prosperous living. To affect a change in your life, change your thinking, first. It may not always be the easiest thing to do, but begin and persist and you will see changes taking place in your life eventually, if not right away.

Regardless of the circumstances in which you may be, you can and should change them into happy, healthy and prosperous ones. Deliberately speaking *Power Words for Prosperous Living,* with *feeling and belief*, will move you into your new life of unlimited riches. They'll help you claim the good you rightfully deserve.

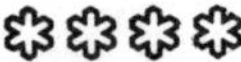

True preparation for wealth is in the mind. Ideas are the coin of the mind realm. Make of your mind the abiding place of rich thoughts. —*Ernest E. Wilson*

Govern the lips as they were palace-doors, the king within; tranquil and fair and courteous be all words which from that presence win. —*Arnold*

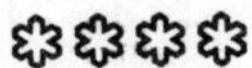

It's Right to be Rich!

It is right, of course, for everyone, especially YOU, to be rich! You should be just as rich as you possibly can. Unfortunately and ignorantly, some people do not believe this due to fear-based religious or parental training.

Regardless of what you may have been taught, *God wants you to be rich,* to enjoy the happy, prosperous life and to do so in an honest way. You should be financially independent so that you may enjoy the good things money can provide, and because it is divinely right for you to be rich.

Granted, *money is not everything, so* **don't** *make a god of it*. Money doesn't guarantee happiness, but money *does* make it easier to have peace of mind, free you to be constructively creative, and to enjoy living in the manner to which you and many others want to be accustomed.

Money is Good!

It is far better to have plenty of money than to have less. Money is good. It is God's good-green-substance! Check up on your attitude towards money. If you have held negative thoughts about it, change them. *Improve your attitude toward money and more of it will flow into your life!*

Money responds to your thoughts about it, and the words you connect to it. Think and speak in an upward, positive way about money. Do not waste your good thought-energy thinking negatively about it. Don't fear it, or the having of too much money. Ask for wisdom and understanding and affirm that money is coming to you now from all directions, and you have the wisdom and intelligence to use it wisely and lovingly.

It is wiser to focus your energy upon your creative ability and use this wisely than to make money the object of your quest. Money will flow when you think right about it, and work within and without to express your creative potential in prospering activity. Rather than being a motivator, let money be a barometer.

BE happy and grateful for the money you have had, have now, and expect to have. Declare that it is flowing into your life in abundant measure now. Affirm: "MONEY IS GOOD. IT IS FLOWING EVER-INCREASINGLY INTO MY LIFE NOW. I USE IT WITH WISDOM AND LOVINGLY PASS IT ON AS IT BLESSES MYSELF AND ALL MANKIND NOW. THANK YOU, FATHER, I AM GRATEFUL."

You have no right to be poor.

Poverty is a sickness and an indication of a conscious separation from God. When there is such a separation in regard to wealth, there is usually a separation in regard to other aspects of living, too. Conscious oneness with God is to be sought after and experienced on a continuing basis. God is within and all around you as the source of all that you are, can have, and experience.

Jesus never condoned poverty. He never decreed that anyone be poor, although he acknowledged the poor would always be around. He said this in recognition of the fact that some people wouldn't learn to use prosperity laws and principles. He did everything He could to convince people to claim, accept and enjoy their rightful inheritance of prosperous living as the deserving children of a loving and infinitely rich Father. He clearly taught and demonstrated "the life more abundant." And He said, "go and do likewise."

Make no excuse for or put up with lack, at least as a permanent condition in your life. Do everything you can, inwardly and outwardly, to eliminate lack from your mind and your life, and to establish yourself in abundance.

Your loving Father-God intends for you to live in a gracious and successful manner. His desire for you is to experience now, daily good health, happiness, peace of mind, harmonious human relationships, and financial plenty. That is true prosperous living—prosperity at its finest!

God has given you everything needed for living the prosperous life. Best of all, He has given you free choice and the POWER OF YOUR SPOKEN WORD. *Choose wisely.*

You and I and everyone should do everything we can to claim and accept our rightful heritage of prosperous living, and help others do the same.

✿✿✿✿

If you spend your life merely in making a living you finally must acknowledge yourself bankrupt in essential wealth . . . Life pays. You name your recompense by what you do, by what you are. —*Imelda Shanklin*

Your "Divine Connection!"

Boldly declaring statements of truth often, with feeling and belief, consciously connects your mind with universal substance within you and everywhere present. This "Divine Connection" makes of you, a mighty avenue through which the universe pours its substance into your life and affairs.

To those who are ignorant of the importance and power of speaking affirmations, it may appear rediculous or of some kind of "magic" to do so, but they do not understand the affirmative process. It seems they would rather remain ignorant—and in lack than to use this scientific prayer way of accepting the riches of the universe.

Don't allow yourself to be influenced by such

negative doubters. While they are doubting, go ahead and prove the power of prosperity affirmations and claim and accept the resulting increasing prosperity and success.

Remember, *it is your mind through which the Infinite's riches pour into your life. They can come in no other way. By making the "Divine Connection" through your prospering words, you open the way for more riches to flow into your life.*

It will seem like "magic"!

There is, of course, "magic" in the spoken word in that it carries such potent prospering power it may seem like "magic" for your dreams to start coming true so much easier. If you are unfamiliar with this special prospering technique, I urge you to give it a sufficient try before you discount it. I am sure, when you understand it and do as instructed, you will see how easy it works and be convinced of the power of speaking prosperity affirmations.

You will have results because you will have made the "Divine Connection" within yourself with the Source of all-good and opened out the way for your rich good to flow. Where you may have been blocking it before, your good will pour copiously into your life for you to enjoy.

The more you make the "Divine Connection" within, the more you will enjoy prosperous living!

I am!

Many affirmations in this book, begin with or include the words, "I am." The reason for this is much more than to just put them in the first person pronoun for your personal use. "I am" is your spiritual identity; the *real* you, the Christ Mind in you. "I am" is your "handle of power" by which you shape your life. It is your "golden key" to infinite riches. Use it wisely!

By the use of "I am" you build up or tear down your life. It is wise to always make positive assertions when making statements, or just thinking, that include "I am."

For instance, it is better to say, "I am happy, healthy and prosperous" than to say, "I am unhappy, sick, or poor." The first is the truth about you; the second is false. You always want to declare that which is truth. To do otherwise is to speak contrary to the reality of your being and the Universe.

It is amazing how many people ignorantly and carelessly use their "I am" power to degrade themselves and avoid the good they might otherwise enjoy. At the same time, many others are wisely using their "I am" power in positive acceptance of themselves as divine creations deserving of God's very best. *Through their "I am" power they are claiming and enjoying prosperous living.*

Use Your "I am" wisely!

It is of real value to you to listen to how you use your "I am." Be mindful that you don't use it in connection with anything you don't want to experience or to be continued in your life. If you have been connecting your "I am" with words that are negative, not true, or not constructive, begin immediately to connect your "I am" with words that are in harmony with the prosperity and happiness you want to experience. *Be wise in your selection of words—spoken or unspoken—to which you attach your "I am."*

There is vast power in "I am." You will experience a pleasant change in yourself and in your life by daily declaring over and over, "I am!" "I am!" "I am!" Do this for several days, speaking the words audibly and meditating upon them silently. Repeat this exercise periodically. It will help you to realize WHO and WHAT you are!

Speak the word for others!

You may use the same "I am" power to bless others with realizations of truth, to help them prosper, by declaring: "You are", "They are", and "We are." Know that what you declare is so. Do not, however, declare anything for another that you would not want in your own life. What you claim for others you are claiming for yourself, just as what you declare for yourself is true for all. Never criticize or condemn anyone. Always speak words that are positive, upward and prospering.

Maintain positive spaces.

Do not engage in worried, anxious or negative thinking or speaking about yourself or others between the times of speaking prosperity affirmations. Keep your faith high and your attitude positive. *Act as though you believe what you have declared is so.* To speak the word and then return to or give energy to making negative assertions, negates the good you have done.

The same thing is true in prayer. When you have prayed, accepting that what you desire is God's desire for you, do not doubt; do not waste time or energy in negative thinking. Your faith is being rewarded. Get out of the way and let God take care of things. *He is!*

Scientific Prayer

Speaking affirmations is scientific prayer—prayer of the highest kind—in that through your "I am" you unify your mind with God-Mind, and thereby bring the best results.

In scientific prayer, you affirm (decree, claim, and thankfully accept) that which is yours by divine right, rather than begging God to give you something if He so chooses or "finds you worthy."

Jesus didn't teach that we should be beggars, but that we are now the deserving children of a loving, rich and benevolent Father, and that we are to claim and accept our divine inheritance of abundant living now.

In understanding faith, use your "I am" power to claim and enjoy your rich good now. *You do not have to beg for what is already yours.*

✲✲✲✲

The mind of each individual may be consciously unified with Divine Mind through the indwelling Christ. By affirming at-one-ment with God-Mind, we eventually realize the perfect mind which was in Christ Jesus. —Charles Fillmore

Do Your Work!

Speak your word (make declarations of truth daily), and persist in doing so. Set aside a specific time for this important exercise and keep it just for that. Your daily affirmative work is essential because you are building prosperity consciousness. You must have the mental equivalent before you can have your desires fulfilled. If you don't realize results immediately, keep on. Persistence will eventually bring your desired good into your life.

However, you will feel something beginning to stir within you, right away. You will feel uplifted as your consciousness moves on to a higher plane of thinking. You know something good is happening in you. What you feel is the activity of Spirit moving in and through you and radiating from you, attracting corresponding substance that clothes the words you speak.

Charge your mind with prospering ideas and words, and you *will have plenty in your world.* Most of all, do not waste your good thought-energy and word-power in negative thinking or speaking. Never talk "hard times." If you do you are sowing "hard times" seed and by the law of sowing and reaping, you will reap a harvest of "hard times." *Sow success and prosperity seeds through your words and you will reap success and prosperity.*

Discard Poverty Words.

You can bring prosperity into your life and home by discarding words that have the idea of poverty in them, and by carefully selecting words that embody the idea of plenty.

Never allow yourself to assert anything, no matter how true it may appear, that you would not want continued or reproduced in your life. Regardless of appearances, never say that money is scarce. Such a thought held in mind, or expressed, will scare money away from you along with many other good things and experiences. It will avoid you and you do not want that.

As stated previously, and worth repeating, money is good and you should do everything you can, in an honest way, to attract money in sufficient quantities so that financial struggle is eliminated and financial ease is enjoyed.

Talk and Think—Plenty!

Myrtle Fillmore, co-founder of Unity, said, "Never say that times are hard with you; these words tighten your purse strings until Omnipotence will be powerless to loosen them. Begin right now to talk plenty, think plenty, give thanks for plenty.

"Turn the great energy of your thought upon 'plenty ideas', and you will have plenty, no matter what people about you are saying. Another thing: You are not to take your prosperity as a matter of fact. You are to be as deeply grateful for every demonstration as you would be for some unexpected treasure poured into your lap." *("How to Let God Help You"—Unity Books)*

Be assured, you will reap desired results when you do your work in faith knowing God is working in you and everywhere doing His part, and in the understanding that your mental and spiritual work is of infinite value and power. *Begin, persist and grow. You are growing into your personal prosperous life!*

✿✿✿✿

You and I must not complain if our plans break down if we have done our part. That means that the plans of One who knows more than we do have succeeded. —Edward E. Hale

Praise and Thanksgiving

One of the surest ways to open the floodgates of prosperity is to sincerely praise and give thanks to God, the source of your wealth, for all the good you have had, all you have now, and all that you expect to have.

If or when things do not go as well as you would like, or if your prosperity seems too slow or even ignores you, examine your thoughts and words to see if you need to be more genuinely grateful, and to raise your voice in words of praise and thanksgiving. If things are going okay and you just want to enjoy more of God's good-green-energy called money, and more of His other rich blessings, increase your praising and thanking activity.

This is not to "con" God, because you can't do that and get away with it, but to free your mental and emotional nature so as to make of yourself a more open and receptive channel through which He may pour His riches.

Priase and thanksgiving frees spiritual energy in you so that you are alive with dynamic energy that radiates from you irresistibly attracting more and more of God's very best for you.

Praise everything in your life.

Praise yourself and give thanks to God that He has given you the wisdom and understanding to prosper. *Praise your talents and abilities*. They will work even better for you when you do. Give thanks for your good mind and for the opportunity to use it to enrich yourself and your loved ones. Look for things to praise and give thanks for. *Count your blessings*. Writing your blessings on paper, making daily lists, is a very beneficial exercise. It not only helps you get your mind away from difficulties, but frees you to attract more rich good into your life.

Give thanks for the little things as well as the larger blessings. Being thankful for small blessings helps bring larger ones. A soul that finds little or nothing to praise or give thanks for, is looking in the wrong direction! Appreciate yourself and all you have and expect to have, and you will soon have more. *Especially praise and give thanks for every little bit of improvement in your life, and you will be amazed at how quickly and easily it grows!*

Bless your challenges.

Be sure to praise and give thanks for your challenges. Look for the good in them. Give thanks for the power in you to overcome every difficulty. When you sincerely bless and give thanks for challenges, they bless you in return rather than sap your energy and hold you in bondage. Sometimes people remain in un-desirable conditions until they learn to find the good in them and praise that good, giving thanks for the challenge that makes them grow.

Praise and gratitude is the very best attitude!

When we hear somebody complaining that he has not enough, we may know that he has not expressed enough appreciation for what he already has. —*Lowell Fillmore*

Mental attitudes more than mental capacities cause our success or our failure.

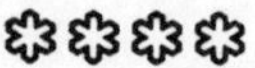

Belief: Your "Golden Key" to Prosperity

One of the fundamental things you should understand about the use of affirmations is: BELIEVE THE WORDS YOU SPEAK ARE TRUE. Regardless of what appearances may seem to tell you, or of what you may have been taught, believe the words you speak are true. The more realization you can put into this practice, the quicker and more satisfying will be your demonstrations.

In reality, you are not speaking the words trying to make something so—you are making your positive assertions in the realization—belief—it is so now. This is true because God has already given to you, all you could ever desire, in spirit, and the speaking of your word is in confirmation of or mental acceptance of that which is yours now.

You want to quicken spiritual substance so that it responds to the words you declare; to the ideas you hold in mind and that your words embody so that it gathers together, so-to-speak, and manifests in your desired rich good. You do not quicken substance through weak or indefinite declarations. You *do* quicken substance through your understanding faith and positive declarations knowing your good is yours now.

The reason there is a need to speak prosperity affirmations is more than to quicken substance. Many people have been making negative assertions for years thus convincing themselves that something other than overflowing prosperity is their lot in life and they just have to accept it. Some people do not believe they are worth much because of inferior self images, therefore they are careless in what they claim and accept. This kind of thinking needs to be upgraded. *Prosperity affirmations are dynamic to change thinking and behavior patterns.*

Develop Prosperous Thinking

To enjoy true prosperous living, you must first develop prosperous thinking. Thinking prosperously is a "golden key" to living the prosperous life! Although what you declare when you speak affirmations is so, you may need to convince your subconscious mind of that. Through your subconscious mind, you make the mystical connection with universal substance, the essence of your wealth.

Just a few prospering words spoken with power and belief, can dispel even years of negative thinking; break up and dislodge a lot of poverty-programming, and propel you forward on a higher plane of prospering activity.

The Universe is basically positive and when you speak positive, prospering words, you are getting your mind and your spiritual nature in harmony with the Universe. The Universe is friendly and wants to prosper you. It wants to help you. Accept this as true and cooperate with it. *No longer allow yourself to stand in the way of your rightful inheritance of unlimited prosperity.*

Your words (prosperity affirmations) are infinitely powerful to transform your life, but it all begins in Mind. Mind is the Master Power that molds your life. Make your affirmations conform to that which is infinitely true and in accord with what you desire to experience, and miracles will happen to you!

For best results, select one or two affirmations which have meaning to you, and speak them over several times. Do this three times daily for several days. Whenever they come to mind during the day, or when negative, doubtful, or other non-prospering thoughts try to enter your mind, speak the affirmations several times again. Then release them and go about your business in an uplifted consciousness.

A very helpful way to use affirmations is to write or print them on 3 x 5 cards. Make the words as large as possible for easy reading. Carry the cards with you. You may also place them on your bathroom mirror, on the refrigerator, the instrument panel of your car, and in other places where you will see them easily and often.

Do not be anxious.

Release all anxiety and worry from your mind. Be as relaxed as you possibly can when you speak affirmations. This doesn't mean to be indifferent, but to have the feeling you know something good is happening even though you cannot see it with your physical eyes. *Believe it is so now.*

Practice the attitude that what you say is so in the realization you are experiencing your desires now. Relax and let it happen. Believe God is working in your behalf taking care of every detail, bringing your desired good into your life now. He is!

Affirmations help you build faith. Faith is the result of many affirmations. Each affirmation you speak or hold in the silence, helps to build up a substantial, firm, and unwavering state of mind because it establishes Truth in your consciousness.

As you learn to use prosperity affirmations as instructed in this book, and use them daily, you will soon be automatically switching your thinking to positive, prospering words instead of allowing yourself to be dragged down into negative, unproductive thinking. You will find new energy that lifts you out of depression and discouragement onto a higher level of positive thinking and action. You'll be happier, healthier, and everything will be easier. You will be amazed at how easy it is for your dreams to come true!

Belief is a "golden key" to prosperous living! This is especially true when you have created in you, a belief system that is pregnant with prospering ideas, energy and activity.

✿✿✿✿

There is but one hand in the universe. It is God's hand. Whenever you have felt that your hand was empty, it has been because you have believed yourself something separate from God. —*H. Emily Cady*

"Silence" Power!

In the Silence there is infinite power for true achievement. Take one, two, or three affirmations into the Silence within you and meditate upon them.

Do this by speaking them over several times as you relax and quiet your mind. Turn consciously within. Relax as deeply as you can and speak the words softly as you let them drift into your inner-most consciousness. Consciously relax and let go. The more relaxed you are, the better. Dwell upon the words (affirmations) in the stillness of your soul until you feel and know, "the Secret place of the Most High."

In that mystical Presence, you know the reality of the words you speak. Having spoken your word several times, be still.

Wait! Listen!

Wait quietly and listen for whatever Infinite Intelligence has for you. It will "speak" through "the still small voice" to your inner-most consciousness when you are still enough and receptive enough. Do not force. Relax, let go, listen and wait patiently, but with high expectation.

Listen, expect rich ideas! The knowing what you have asked for by affirming it is so, will be full in you. Consciously dwell in this realization. By this process you are building true prosperity consciousness that must express itself through you and in your life as prosperous living.

In effect, you have programmed your subconscious mind for what you wish to experience in your life. You have made the "Divine Connection" so that the Infinite may pour His riches out for you through you. The more you make of yourself a clear, open avenue through which universal substance may flow, the easier and greater will be the good manifesting in your life.

Be Grateful!

Genuine gratitude in the Silence is of immense value.

After relaxing, waiting and listening in the Silence for a time, no matter what happens, lovingly give thanks and take this consciousness into the things you have to do. This dynamic power will move you into new avenues of more productive and prospering activity.

❁❁❁❁

Silence is the key that unlocks the vast resources of the Universe.

❁❁❁❁

All is in the Silence waiting to be brought
Forth to form and substance by the builder, Thought,
That is how God fashioned everything He Wrought,
Everything you long for, in the Silence wait,
Yours the power to shape them either soon or late,
But be very careful how you form your fate.

—Ella Wheeler Wilcox

Writing Power!

There is substantial power in writing out two or three affirmations at least fifteen times daily. Do this for several days and you will experience a positive change in your consciousness (thinking and feeling), and things will begin to change in your life, too.

There is something mystical and powerful about writing affirmations. It serves to focus your mind upon a given point of thought thus presenting to your subconscious mind, correct information and drawing out of Infinite Intelligence, the faith-substance that prospers you.

After writing two or three affirmations for a few days, go on to others that have special meaning to you. An important thing to remember in the use of affirmations is, they become an integral part of you. After awhile you may not need to use particular affirmations again because they have become part of your belief system. It is what you *believe to be true* that manifests in your life as the experiences you have, and the things you enjoy.

Affirmations release prospering energy!

Writing or speaking affirmations release mighty spiritual energy in your consciousness that makes of you an irresistible magnet. This energy radiates from you gathering substance, as it were, to you, along with people and things to prosper you.

The practice of writing is of particular benefit to those who do not care to speak affirmations. Some peole find this easier and more meaningful than speaking affirmations audibly. If this is so for you, by all means write out your affirmations. Or, if you like to speak affirmations, you will find much added power in writing them, too.

Persistence in doing either or both is essential, however, for success.

✿✿✿✿

Instead of giving up to circumstances and outer events we should remember that we are all very close to a kingdom of mind that would make us always happy and successful if we would cultivate it and make it and its laws part of our life.

—Charles Fillmore

Another prospering technique!

Do not under-estimate the power and benefit of just reading prosperity affirmations. Although it may not seem as powerful as speaking or writing prosperity affirmations, this is of substantial power and helps immeasurably to program your mind for prosperous living. You will find it of special value to read several affirmations over a few times and then take them into the Silence with you, and meditate upon them. Focus your thinking upon the ideas contained in the affirmations.

As you read, think about what they really mean and allow them to enter easily into your thinking process. You may enhance your reading by selecting just a few affirmations and read them several times daily, for a few days. This, too, serves to impress your subconscious mind with true ideas. Daily giving your subconscious correct information is very beneficial and brings desired results.

Feed your mind with prospering ideas.

Everything you do to feed your mind with prospering ideas makes it that much easier for you to experience continually increasing prosperity. You will find it helpful to keep copies of this book in handy places for quick reference, such as, by your bed for evening and morning use—just before going to sleep, and upon awakening. There is added benefit and power in focusing upon and reading or speaking affirmations just before sleep, and upon awakening. Your subconscious mind doesn't sleep and will work on what you present to it, through the night. Re-affirmation in the morning prepares you for a more prosperous day.

Keep copies of this book in your car, on your desk, and in other places where you may use it often.

Do all you can to fill your mind with prospering ideas. Saturate it with the ideas in this book, and use other materials that help you prosper. This will help you to ward off negatives thrown your way via radio, TV, other people, and those that come up from your own thinking. *The more you charge your mind with prospering ideas, the happier, healthier, and more financially independent you are.*

Don't hurry!

It is understandable that someone who has been experiencing less than the unlimited prosperity they desire and should have, may be very eager to change things. However, it is wise to not hurry. If you have spent years in negatively programming your mind with lack-producing thoughts and words; if you have not experienced a really high level of prosperous living, you should understand it may take some time to change your thinking sufficiently so that it begins to make a positive difference in your life.

Sometimes, when I have worked with people to help them improve their lives; to change from struggle and lack to ease and abundance, after a little while, some tend to lose patience and their faith wanes. (Of course, their faith was not very strong to begin with or they would have been demonstrating a much better level of prosperity in their lives.) It is then they may want to quit, saying, "It doesn't work."

Usually this is the case when a person has been living in financial desperation and he is desperate to get more money coming in. This desperation seems to be carried over into the new affirmative activity.

It is understandable, of course, that someone who has struggled to "make ends meet", may be over zealous in his efforts to get into a much more satisfying prosperity bracket. Most of the people I have worked with, who have been lack-prone, are very eager to get out of it. When they learn they can, and how to do it, it usually doesn't take them long to get busy doing as instructed! They're ready for prosperity and want to get on with it, and should!

However, I caution them to not try to hurry their good and to not lose faith or become discouraged if things do not improve immediately, or as fast as they think it should.

Don't give up!

Just when you might think of giving up, that may be the time when your rich good is about to come to you. A little more persistence is sometimes all that is needed to bring results. This has been my experience many times.

It is good to remember, that with every affirmation you speak you are building prosperity consciousness and substance is gathering and building up. When the time is right, when your consciousness is filled enough with prospering substance, it will overflow into your life. Make no mistake about this! *And, the longer your good is in coming, the larger and grander it will be!*

I used to get discouraged with the apparent slowness of my richer good and would tend to give up until I learned that substance was gathering and to persist in my effort. Building my faith through continuing to speak prosperity affirmations, I confidently relaxed and let go knowing God was taking care of things. He has never failed to come through, and always on time!

Actually, God has everything already worked out. He is ready when you are. And, when you are ready, His rich good will pour into your life. It may not come as a flood, at first, but come it will! Give thanks for every little bit of improvement and move on with an air of expectancy.

Every thought you think or hold in the Silence, and every word you speak, has some affect upon your subconscious mind and subsequently upon your life. Granted, it may seem imperceptible but, YOUR THOUGHTS AND WORDS *DO* MAKE A DIFFERENCE!

If you are well-acquainted with the affirmative process, then you know how effective affirmations are. If you have not used this method, then give it a chance to work. *Do not lose heart. Keep on!*

After more than twenty-five years of using affirmations, I know they work. They are powerful and always bring results. They will work for you, too, when you use them as directed—with *feeling, belief, and acceptance.*

Relax!

Hurry blocks your way. Hurry implies fear, and fear is definitely a psychological block that will keep your good from you. To hurry is to try to force. What you actually do, is force your good *away* from you.

In reality, what you want to do is to quicken spiritual substance in and around you; to make of yourself a force field of prospering energy that radiates from you. This magnetizes your good, drawing it to you.

Remember: It is prosperous thinking that results in prosperous living. Being anxious, worried, or in a hurry, is **not** *prosperous thinking.*

Prospering words (affirmations) are your tools by which you quicken spiritual substance and charge your thought process with prospering energy. Spoken with power and authority, with realization and acceptance, affirmations are extremely powerful to move universal substance. It will move right into your life in the form of financial abundance.

Patience is rewarded

Do your work and relax in the realization your good is already on its way to you, and in truth, it is with you now. It is always where you are. It has never been away from you. Although you may not be able to see it with your physical eyes, never-the-less, it is there. It is perceived through your understanding faith. Turn consciously within and be still enough and you will know.

Being patient doesn't mean you must wait a long time. It does mean that as you are doing your inner and outer work, you understand that substance is gathering and at the right moment, it will manifest in your life.

Patience and persistence are two requisites for achieving the success and prosperity you want. Do your work knowing you deserve the very best

God has to give. Hold yourself in a high and confident consciousness while expecting to receive knowing you are now receiving, and you will be amazed at what happens!

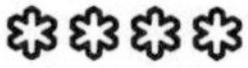

Persistence changes a man's character as carbon changes brittle iron to invincible steel. With persistence you develop a magical quotient of money consciousness, and your subconscious mind is at work continuously to get the money you require.

—Napoleon Hill

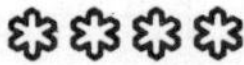

Amid all the mysteries by which we are surrounded nothing is more certain than that we are ever in the presence of an Infinite and Eternal Energy from which all things proceed.

—Herbert Spencer

Now!

Regardless of how long it may seem to take to demonstrate your desired prosperity, it will be NOW when you do. There is no time other than NOW. Even the last moment has gone, and the next is not here yet. Do not try to live in either!

What you are doing NOW is of the most importance. You cannot go back and un-do something done yesterday, so don't try. You cannot live tomorrow so don't try to do that, either. The most important time you have and the only time you have is, NOW. That is why it is always right to speak your affirmations in the realization of "NOW."

You do not want your good some indefinite time in the future. Although it may seemingly take some time for the affirmative process to show any real effect, believe that what you are declaring is so NOW.

Don't put off your good!

Some people tend to put off their good by thinking and speaking in terms of "some day" or "sometime" or "maybe." They believe it is going to take a lot of time, energy and work to achieve their goals, if ever, but this is not necessarily true. And regardless of how long it may seem to take, it will be NOW when your good arrives. Speak in terms of "NOW." Do this until you have changed "future"-thinking to "NOW"-thinking.

This does not imply impatience or hurry. It *does* help you to realize that God is right where you are now, and since He is the source of your rich supply, your rich good is where you are NOW. Also, your subsconscious mind only knows and can act NOW, and when you do demonstrate your desired good, it is always NOW when you experience it.

Not "some day"—"NOW!"

I am sure you would not want to speak an affirmation such as, "I give thanks for my increased prosperity some day." Or even, "tomorrow", or "next week", etc. You would want to declare with thankful acceptance: "I give thanks for my increasing prosperity NOW!"

In speaking your affirmation in this way, you are confirming the truth that your prosperity is actually increasing now (which it surely is), and you do not have to wait until some indefinite time in the future.

Even though you may not see any visible signs, you KNOW and accept your prosperity as yours NOW, and relax and do what needs doing by you to help make it a reality in your life. You go about your business KNOWING the whole Universe is working on it. This is understanding faith, the kind that moves mountains and produces prospering results.

Right now, right where you are, prospering substance awaits your spoken word. Move it into your life through speaking prosperity affirmations NOW, in the realization your rich good is yours NOW. It is!

✿✿✿✿

How much can one demonstrate? Just what one can believe. How much can we see, how much can we accept, how much can we find in our consciousness that is no longer repudiated by our own denials? Whatever that is, that much we can have. —*Ernest Holmes*

Do Your Part!

You understand, by now, how wise and beneficial it is to speak Power Words for Prosperous Living. However, it is equally wise and beneficial for you to *MOVE IN THE DIRECTION OF YOUR GOALS*. Do everything you can to help establish yourself in prosperous living, and your success will be easier, faster and more satisfying.

Of course, when you use the affirmations in this book, as instructed, you will be moved to take action. You will be alive with new energy and ideas. You will be enthusiastically busy doing everything you can to get into your higher prospering experience.

Action is Affirmation!

When you believe in your goals, yourself, and the positive power within you, and have generated sufficient faith through speaking prosperity affirmations, you will act as though you believe what you declare. You will, in effect, give "feet" and "legs" to your spoken word and step boldly forth in faith confidently acting upon your goals. *As powerful as affirmations are, it is moving in the direction of your goals that move them toward you!*

I have two bicycles. On one I don't go anywhere. On the other I may ride for miles and often ride it to my office. One is a stationary exercise bike. The other is a ten-speed touring bike. On the exercise bike I may peddle for all I'm worth for a long time. So far, it has not moved an inch, yet this activity is very beneficial. When I get on my ten-speed, I move along the streets and soon arrive at my destination.

Both bikes are beneficial, but it is the movement toward a destination—a goal—that is more satisfying. It is the forward movement that is important!

The same is true with you. Speak your word and then move forward in the realization, what you say is so now. Speaking power words is excellent exercise and extremely beneficial, but it is the action you take in an outer way, that moves you and your goal together.

Act as though it is already so!

If you believe it is so, act that way! Action, stepping boldly forth, helps to bolster your faith and give you confidence. A favorite saying of mine is, "ACT AS THOUGH IT IS ALREADY SO." This is confidence of the highest kind—the kind that assures you, you are on the right track and your good is yours now.

If you have been desiring healing, act as though you are already healed. If you have been wanting greater happiness, act that way, and for substantially increased income, act as though it has already happened. Do this, especially with specific goals. Clearly visualize your goals in your imagination and then act as though they are already yours now. In reality, they are!

There is great power in this to convince your subconscious mind that you mean business, and that you do want to actually live the prosperous life, and you will accept nothing less. Also, this generates an abundance of positive energy within you that moves you into prospering activity, which in turn, produces desired results.

When you do your part, God never fails to do His. Speaking power words and working in an outer way toward your goals, is making yourself harmonize with the Great Affirmative.

Doing your part is belief, in action! If you believe it—do it!

✽✽✽✽

Winning is a state of mind as well as a historical fact. You can't achieve the historical fact unless you first achieve the state of mind in which you have faith that you will win. Gamblers and athletes put it this way: "People who think like winners win." That doesn't mean that winning is inevitable if you think you're going to win. However, it enables you to do a better job, and makes victory more likely. No one wins all the time. But if you believe you're going to lose, then you're defeated before you start; you then inevitably lose.

—Charleston Heston

Goals! Goals! Goals!

If you are really serious about achieving a very comfortable level of prosperous living, you will know, goal setting is of utmost importance. You know it is an integral part of living in a positive and successful manner.

We are goal-striving beings by nature, and we need goals to work on; to strive toward so we do not become unbalanced. Since you desire increased prosperity; to live the prosperous life, have you determined just how prosperous you want to be? Have you decided upon a weekly, monthly, or annual income figure? What kind of things do you want in your life which will be your indicators of prosperous living? *You cannot afford to be vague about this.*

The more in-expensive way is to have a clear idea of how much prosperity you want to actually experience. You need to know exactly what it is you want so you may give definite direction to your subconscious mind. Decide. Do not be hazy concerning this.

Muddled, confused direction can only produce muddled, confused results. Mediocre thinking brings mediocre results. Positive, definite thinking and direction produce positive, definite and highly desirable results. Decide on what you want and determine you will have that—or something better.

Write your goals!

When you have made your goal-decision, write it down on paper. This cannot be emphasized enough. It is of immeasurable value to you and directly related to your success in achieving your goals. ***Write your goals down on paper!***

First, of course, you must have goals. Most people have desires and even more have wishes. However, it is the people who understand the importance of goals and of writing them down, who are the real achievers. The others often just drift and wonder why life doesn't give them more.

Choose your direction

Upon asking a teenager, who had recently graduated from high school, what she planned to do with her life, she replied, "I'm just leaving it to the Lord." Well, that is admirable, as far as it goes, because everyone should seek divine guidance for their lives. However, the Lord wants to know the direction you want to go. That is why you were given freedom of choice and a mind to use to make of your life what you will.

Believe me, *if you don't take dominion, and direct your own life, someone else will, and you may not like that at all!*

Sometimes, when a person says something to indicate they are "leaving it to the Lord," it is just a "cop-out" in that they don't want to take responsibility for their lives, are ignorant of the tremendous power of their minds, or are just too lazy to really think and act in an upward, successful manner.

"The Lord helps those who help themselves," is an old saying with a lot of truth in it. I discovered many years ago, that when I just left everything to the Lord, so-to-speak, not much of any real value got done through me. At least, what was done was usually through hard, personal struggle. When I learned to work in harmony with spiritual laws and principles; to use scientific prayer by using affirmations, accept and invoke the power of God within myself, things went very much better. Much more was accomplished without the struggle and hard work. It continues to get better with each passing day.

Ask! Seek! Knock!

If you have not been setting definite goals, and most of all, if you have not been writing them down, then get busy and find out for yourself just how practical and dynamic this is. The Lord (the Christ; the creative power within you) wants to know the direction you wish to go. If you want His guidance, ask for it. *Ask! Seek! Knock!* Divine guidance will be given you. Then make your goal-decisions accordingly. *Write them down on paper and then get busy doing everything you can to achieve them.*

Writing your goals down on paper puts them before you where you may review them often, but more importantly, they are set in your mind. If you tend to wander away from your goals, having them written helps you keep on track. *Reading your goals each day helps bring ideas, energy and substance for fulfilling your goals.*

If you say you have goals but do not write them down, you are probably just fooling yourself. You really haven't made up your mind to actually have them in your life. Or, believe you can and will have them.

Make up your mind!

You know how easy it is to think of something you may want to achieve, and you may even get a good picture of it in your mind, but some time later, something distracts you and you forget all about it. Our minds are very busy with millions of thoughts flowing through, daily. There are a multitude of inner and outer influences. That is why it is important to decide what you want to achieve and write it down on paper.

Once you have decided on a goal, go after it with all your heart. Act as though it is yours now. Speak your word (prosperity affirmations) in accord with your goals, and act in harmony with them. Use your imagination to clearly visualize your goals as yours now.

When do you want your goals?

In determining and writing your goals, decide WHEN you want to achieve them. Write the date alongside your goals. This serves to set a time limit and to get you moving toward what you want to achieve. However, it doesn't greatly matter if you do not achieve your goals on time. Yet it does serve to move you to greater action inwardly and outwardly.

I am not implying that a goal-date is unimportant, or that you should be indifferent toward achieving your goals on time. On the contrary, you should do all you can to achieve them when you say you want them, and expect to have them.

If things don't work out by the date you have set, don't get discouraged and by all means don't give up! Re-set the date and make a new determination you will have your goals—on time!

Remove the blocks!

It is very helpful to examine your thoughts, feelings, words, and actions in relation to your goals. Take a good look at your inner-most thoughts. Do you really want your goals? Do you believe you can have them? Do you believe you are deserving? Are there any subtle, or deep-seated feelings or beliefs that might block your good such as: anger, resentment, unforgiveness of self or others, or low self-esteem? Are you in a hurry? Can you really accept yourself enjoying prosperous living?

Are you giving sufficient time and energy without over-efforting, to doing the positive thing? Are you creating within yourself the positive mental environment required for living the prosperous life? Are you actually doing all you can, inwardly and outwardly, to achieve your goals?

Do not, however, spend too much time in introspection, at least, don't get bogged down in negatives. Use your energy to focus upon the positives and what you want to achieve. Remember: *You have many more pluses than minuses!*

It's good to remember, too, the Universe can only give you what you are willing to—and *do* accept. *Acceptance is a "golden key" to actually having in your life, the desires of your heart.*

Divinely directed, choose your goals and write them down on paper. Visualize them clearly in your imagination, use affirmations in line with your goals, do all you can, and gratefully accept them as yours now. *They are!*

You can get rid of any difficulty whatever from your life as soon as you love God more than you love error.

—Emmet Fox

The poorest of all men is not one without gold, but without a goal. Life to him has no meaning—no reason for living.

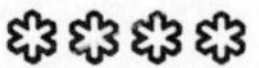

Keep Your Goals Private!

Secrecy holds dynamic power! The more you keep your goals and plans to yourself—thinking about them and working on them secretly—the greater is the power generated in you for real achievement.

People who are outstandingly successful; who accomplish more than the average person, do not talk about what they want to do—they do it—letting others see what they had in mind.

Your goals are *your* business and *only* yours. *Be very careful with whom you talk to about your goals while you are working on them.* Do NOT share them with anyone unless you are certain that person is able to, and will assist you in achieving your goals. It is far better to work quietly on your goals and let other people see them when you have achieved them than to just talk and not achieve them.

Those who do a lot of talking about their goals, often have as their goals the impressing of other people with how talkative they are instead of how industrious and successful they are through actual achievements.

When you know what you want and are confidently taking positive action toward your goals, assured of success, it is amazing how, without saying a word to anyone, other people come along to help. Also, ideas and materials just seem to find their way to you! This is because the positive energy you generate by being goal-directed, acts as irresistible attracting power that draws to you, help from every direction.

There is something powerful and good about a goal-directed person! This is especially true when you know what you want, have a plan for achieving it, and keep quiet about it.

Your unlimited creative potential.

Your help really comes from within you. You have unlimited creative potential for making your desires actualities in your life. God gave it to you, and keeps on giving. In truth, He is your unlimited creative potential and He is within you, as you! He has created you for success, and equipped you to express health, happiness, peace of mind, and to live the prosperous life.

You are far more than you appear to be. You are a spiritual being endowed with infinite spiritual qualities and ability.

You are a walking "gold mine!" Your success and prosperity will overflow in your life in wonderful abundance when you "dig out" the "gold" within you.

"This or something better!"

When you have written your goals on paper, "burn your bridges behind you." Determine you will have these goals (or something better). Leave no stone unturned until you have accomplished what you have set before you. Speaking of "something better," it is wise to add to your goals, "this or something better, Father," when writing your goals. In this way you leave the door open, so-to-speak, for God to give you His very best.

Do not bog yourself down in small thinking. Too often people do not ask large enough. Be sure to expand your thinking and your imagination and faith when setting goals. Lift your personal estimate of yourself—not in an egotistical way, but in the realization of who and what you are as a deserving, loved, infintely endowed child of God—a divine expression of Him.

Unfortunately, some people have been taught to believe they are not worth or deserve much, and often feel guilty if they happen to receive even a little. Consequently, they don't ask for much and are often timid about doing even that.

Ask largely and **expect** *to receive what you ask for.* You cannot ask for too much, and besides, it's good mental exercise to expand your thinking into larger orbits of achievement. This makes you grow and to use your creative power.

You simply cannot become a millionarie on hundred-dollar thinking. If being a millionaire is in your plans, very quietly see and accept yourself as that now, and think more largely than you have ever thought before.

If you have been thinking too small, stop! Change your mind and keep it changed. Expand your thinking, enlarge your desires. Accept that you are deserving of God's best—in abundance—with no questions asked.

The "GOALden Achiever"©

A dynamic help in goal-achieving, is the "GOALden Achiever."© I use one daily, along with thousands of other goal-directed people. I designed it to specifically help you decide on your goals and to achieve them. (You may have a "GOALden Achiever"© by writing to me at P.O. Box 1463-PW, Mesa, AZ 85201 USA)

Ten!

Essential to prosperous living, always give back to God, the source, at least 10% of all you receive. This is called tithing. It is an ancient prosperity principle and practice that is just as valid today as it was centuries ago. If you are a tither, then you know this and quickly agree, this is a definite requirement for living the prosperous life.

Those persons who are prosperous in the truest sense, know the value of "ten" in relation to prosperity and success. They know that "ten" is the mystical number of increase used so successfully by people of every era. This is because tithing makes you a financial partner with God, and you couldn't have a more affluent and dependable Partner! *He has resources which He has placed at your disposal that you cannot begin to imagine or use up.*

Sowing and reaping

Tithing is more than a "financial arrangement" with God. It is proving the law of sowing and reaping, and that you know God as your rich source of never-failing supply. Giving back to the Source, just as the farmer gives back the best seed to the ground, is your recognition of His omnipresent bounty and your way of saying, "Thank You, Father."

Tithing is an excellent way of helping to make the "Divine Connection" with universal riches. "Ten" eliminates much of the hard work many people often connect with success and prosperity. Through "ten" all strain and struggle of prosperous living is avoided. It helps, more than anything, to make your prosperity permanent as well as large, rather than fleeting and small.

A faithful, voluntary tither knows he has a "divine connection" with God, the source of his wealth. He knows he is always divinely protected, and even if some doors seem closed, better ones open. If there are challenges, he knows things will work out and he will be better off than before.

You won't find a tither in the poorhouse. That is because it creates within the person who faithfully tithes, the consciousness of plenty. It is this consciousness of plenty that expresses as plenty in his life and affairs, and it will do the same for you.

If you think you cannot afford to tithe, think again. You really cannot afford *not* to tithe. The reason you may have been struggling financially, is because you have not yet taken God as your financial Partner through tithing. If you have been putting off tithing because you have bills to pay, put God first through tithing and the bills will be easier to pay. Not only that, you will be pleasantly surprised with how much you have left over and how far it goes!

A businessman struggled financially until he learned of "ten" and how it prospers all who apply this prosperity principle. Tithing at least ten percent from his gross income, he was soon on the road to financial plenty and the old struggle and strain became a thing of the past. He declared often: TEN IS THE MYSTICAL NUMBER OF INCREASE. THROUGH MY FAITHFUL TITHING, MY SUCCESS AND PROSPERITY IS GROWING IN AMAZING WAYS NOW. I AM GRATEFUL!

The practicality and efficacy of "ten"—of tithing regularly and consistently when you receive—can be summed up in just two words: ***It works!***

*(You may have a free copy of **"How to Quicken and make Permanent Your Prosperity"** by writing to me at: P.O. Box 1463, Mesa, AZ 85201 USA)*

I hold it true that thoughts are things,
Endowed with being, breath and wings,
And that we send them forth to fill
The world with good results or ill.
—Edwards

❁❁❁❁

The absolute Truth is, there is no lack anywhere, but an overflowing abundance of every kind of good which man can possibly desire or conceive of. *—H. Emily Cady*

❁❁❁❁

A special word of appreciation. I am very grateful for the many friends whose love and tithes have helped me establish the Golden Key Ministry; who financially support our Prayer Ministry and Newsletter. Thank you for your past financial giving, and for all you continue to give.

—John Wolcott Adams

Love!

With all the speaking of prospering words (affirmations), goal setting, utmost faith, and working toward your goals, LOVE is the most important.

Love, in reality, is the very essence of the words you speak or hold in the Silence, and must be the foundation of all that you undertake. *Love is your best "golden key" to prosperous living.*

Without love you are nothing and what you do accounts for little and has no real foundation or substance. Words spoken without love are just words and often meaningless. With love, you are everything and the words you speak are alive with creative potential and positive power. What you do adds up to something real because you have put under your activity the solid substance of love, the reality of the universe and what you are.

Charge your goals with Love!

Love makes your dreams come true; causes you to move into the prosperous life in grand style. As I stated in my book, "BE What You Are: LOVE", "If you really want your dreams to come true, love is the way of fulfillment on a high level. It is the essence of everything worthwhile . . . The truth is, if you really want your prayers answered; to achieve your goals, to be truly happy and successful in a big way, then give your goals a big charge of love and keep on giving it!" *(page 13)*

Love frees you to prosper!

Love frees you from fear. Fear holds too many people in bondage to lack and limitation. By generating love you experience freedom from fear and all of its ugly forms of expressions such as, worry, anger, anxiety, condemnation, guilt, hate, resentment, and small thinking. *Love gives you the power and energy for successful, prosperous living.*

The more you focus on love, and consciously invoke love in all you think, feel, say and do, the happier, healthier, more peaceful and prosperous you are. It may not be true with you, but with many people there is a lack of love in their lives. They seem to have more fear than love. It is fear that binds. It is love that sets you free!

Forgiveness prospers you!

Forgiveness is love expressed. It is identifying with the idea of love instead of fear, hate and resentment; of allowing yourself to be immersed in the true substance of love that makes all things right.

You cannot afford to hurt yourself through anger and unforgiveness. Do not under-estimate the damage and cost of these destructive emotions. You *can afford* to love, bless and forgive. This will pay you rich dividends that will keep on paying interest.

How unfortunate that some people, after being slighted or offended by others, sometimes spend years in ill-health and financial lack because they refuse to forgive and release. It seems they would rather hang on to hurts than be happy, free and prosperous.

Unforgiveness is a form of fear. *Fear has no place in living the prosperous life,* because to be truly prosperous means to express love fully. Love is the way of letting go of fear. "Forgiving is a cleansing and releasing process that unblocks the flow of peace and success energy. We must let grudges and guilt and anger go no matter how fond we have become of these destructive habits." *(p. 6, "BE What You Are: LOVE"—Golden Key Publications.)*

Unblock your prosperity

If something seems to be blocking your prosperity, search within yourself to see if there might be someone (including yourself) or some thing you need to release through forgiveness. Quietly and sincerely forgive everyone and everything and be at peace. Send love to those whom you may have condemned. Give love to yourself. For anything and everything, quickly and completely forgive yourself.

Dwell upon love and the freeing, fulfilling power of love, letting it be in you, that which is real. In short, consciously *BE* What You Are! When you do this, you open the channels for your rich good to fly on wings to you!

Love brings happy change!

One time an office worker experienced difficulty getting along with her fellow workers. Everyone seemed to be against her until she examined her thoughts and feelings. She discovered that she was holding on to little gripes and irritations. She kept computing these in her memory until she hated where she worked and wanted out.

Fortunately, she wised up before the company could fire her. She began loving herself, sending love to her co-workers, and quickly and quietly forgave everyone, including herself. In just a matter of weeks, she noticed a change in the people in her office, and wondered about this until she remembered that she had changed *her* thinking, ceasing from harsh, critical thoughts. It was amazing how the others responded to her new, loving and forgiving attitude.

She said things began to change when she started declaring daily, "DIVINE LOVE IS MY REAL NATURE. I RADIATE LOVE. DIVINE LOVE IS MY FORGIVING POWER AND THE HARMONY OF THIS OFFICE NOW. LOVE IS PROSPERING ME MIGHTILY NOW."

Later, she reported that love was continuing to make her life happier and more prosperous than ever before. She was radiant with health, peace and love, and found it so much easier to give back to God, at least ten percent of her gross income in grateful appreciation of all He was giving her.

There is no substitute for love. As the late Dr. Emmet Fox pointed out, "If you could love enough you would be the happiest and most powerful being in the world." *("The Golden Gate")*

When you love enough, you really do not have to forgive because you do not criticize or condemn, and you do not attract negative people or experiences to you. However, if they do find their way into your life, always quickly and quietly forgive them. *The best thing is to* **love them first.**

BE what you want to attract into your life and you will find success and happiness. You are Love. BE What You Are.

(Forgiveness is more thoroughly covered in my book, "BE What You Are: LOVE.")

Love's on the highroad,
Love's on the byroad—
Love's on the meadow,
and Love's in the mart!

And down every byway
Where I've taken my way,
I've met Love a-smiling—
for Love's in my heart!
—Dana Burnet

Love is a harmonizing, constructive power. When it is made active in consciousness, it conserves substance and reconstructs, rebuilds, and restores man and his world.
—Charles Fillmore

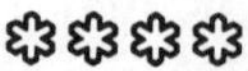

How to use Power Words for Prosperous Living

This book is not one you just read, put down, and forget about. If you do, you will have participated in only a very small part of its intended purpose. This is a prosperity consciousness-building book. Its real purpose is to be a continuing guide and inspiration to you—to be a handy reference for practical help and definite prosperous results.

By using this book as instructed, you will build the consciousness of prosperity that must result in prosperous living for you and your loved ones. This book wants to be your friend. Friends are helpful. It is my desire that this book become one of the most helpful friends you will ever have. Let it help you every day to achieve your goals, to create true prosperity consciousness, and enjoy the success, happiness, good health and prosperity you so rightly deserve, and should have.

You will find it of maximum benefit to do these things:

1. Select one, two, or more affirmations of special meaning to you, or that pertain to your goals.

2. Declare them audibly several times. Also hold them in the Silence, and write them down. 3 x 5 cards are good for writing affirmations on.

3. Use the same affirmations for at least one day before going on to others. You will experience special benefit by using the same affirmation(s) for 30 days, or longer.

4. Speak your word (affirmations) with feeling and belief. Faith is essential.

5. Visualize what you declare, along with your goals, as clearly as you can—with *you* in the picture.

6. Accept what you declare as so now. Accept your goals as yours now.

7. Think, speak, and act "NOW." Really focus on "NOW" not in an anxious way, but in the realization your rich good *is* yours now.

8. Act as though it is already so. It is!

9. Don't hurry. Patience and persistence will reward you richly! Hurry is fear. Patience and persistence are love and faith.

10. Give "feet" and "legs" to your Power Words by doing all you can, inwardly and outwardly.

11. Lovingly and gratefully give back to God at least 10% of your gross income, regularly and consistently in understanding faith and love.

12. LOVE! Love is the true substance of you and your prosperity.

✽✽✽✽

Suggest prosperity to yourself. See yourself in a prosperous condition. Affirm that you will before long be in a prosperous condition. Affirm it calmly and quietly but strongly and confidently. Believe it, believe it absolutely. Expect it—keep it continually watered with expectation. You thus make yourself a magnet to attract the things that you desire. Don't be afraid to suggest, to affirm these things, for by so doing you put forth an ideal which will begin to clothe itself in material form. —*Ralph Waldo Trine*

✽✽✽✽

Power Words for Prosperous Living!

Now, dare to prosper! Boldly declare these powerful prospering truths.

Claim your rich good now! Dare to enjoy Prosperous Living now!

As the rich child of a loving Father, I am open and receptive to His vast good for me now.

I make room to receive. I am doing my part.

Thank You, Father, for Your lavish supply overflowing in beautiful ways in my life and affairs now.

I turn the Golden Key: Turn away from the problem and turn to God.

God in me, is infinite Life, Love, Wisdom, Power, Substance, and All-Good.

Gratefully, I accept His vast rich good overflowing in avalanches of prospering miracles in my life now.

With a thankful heart, I am open and receptive to the vast riches God has for me now.

In faith, I claim and accept my rich good and it is overflowing in avalanches of bountiful blessings in my life now.

I believe I receive. Thank You, God, for answered prayer!

Thank You, God, for your lavish riches overflowing in beautiful blessings in my life now. I am grateful!

The Universal floodgates of Prosperity burst open wide, pouring lots of money into my life now!

God is within me now, as infinite peace and love.

God is within me now, as my all-providing, unlimited supply.

Thank You, God, for peace, love and rich ideas.

Thank You, God, for my growing rich consciousness and for unlimited riches in my life now.

I now release all unforgiving, non-prospering thoughts and feelings from my mind and heart.

I am now free to prosper and I am prospering in rich and wonderful ways now.

Thank You, God, for your lavish supply pouring into my life in rich abundance now.

❁❁❁❁

Thank You, God, for my wonderful Subconscious mind.

I now program my Subconscious mind with positive, prospering thoughts, words and ideas.

I am alert and allow only that which is positive and good to enter in.

Through speaking positive, prospering words, I now program my Subconscious mind with happy, positive, loving, and constructive ideas.

Through my Subconscious mind, I am guided in ways of love, joy, peace, health, and abundant prosperity now.

Through my Subconscious mind, Infinite Intelligence now guides me in ways of love, peace, joy, and prosperity in overflowing measure.

Infinite Intelligence now working through my Subconscious mind, pours rich, lavish, elegant prosperity into my life and affairs now.

Thank You, Father, for my marvelous subconscious mind.

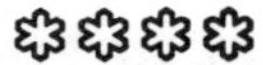

Infinite Intelligence always gives me correct information and opens doors of success and prosperity to me.

Divinely guided, I am always in the right place at the right time and I am prospered easily and abundantly now. I am grateful!

Thank You, God, for Your Presence, Power, and Substance always permeating my mind, body, life and affairs. I am grateful!

I claim and accept my rich good now. I am grateful!

I now relax, let go and listen to the "voice" of Infinite Intelligence "speaking" within me.

My guidance is sure. I know what to do and I do it.

Inspired by the Christ within, I desire the very best God has to give.

I allow my desire for the Good Life to be strong, sustaining and deeply motivating.

I prove my faith by doing everything I can to make my dreams come true.

God in me is invincible, victorious power. The mark of Success is upon me!

✼✼✼✼

Quietly, I meditate upon and accept that money is a divine idea in the Mind of God...that it is good.

I like money and money likes me. It loves to circulate freely and abundantly in my life now.

My right attitude toward money makes me a "money magnet."

Divinely guided, I do the right thing and cause a constant, rich flow of Substance-energy, called money, in my life now.

I am grateful for Plenty! Plenty! Plenty!

✼✼✼✼

God in me, now moves me to greater and greater, more satisfying achievement.

I am open, receptive, and responsive now, to divine direction and guidance. I follow this guidance and DO as instructed.

I now let God's Creative Intention for me, have full and free expression.

I ask, I listen, I follow through. My success is assured.

❁❁❁❁

I am now a TEN TIMES thinker: Ten times healthier, ten times happier and ten times wealthier!

My new attitude now attracts ten times more of God's infinite good into my life.

I am now ten times more grateful!

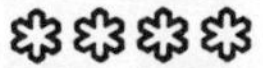

Thinking makes the difference. I now think on prospering ideas.

Infinite Intelligence now guides me in right-thinking for prosperity and happiness.

I now claim and accept the unlimited abundance of all good things that are mine by divine right.

Freely and gratefully, I share with others the prospering truth, and my rich supply.

With faith in God, I now set my goals high and move toward them totally confident of success.

God, in me, is everything I need to realize my goals. He loves, guides, and prospers me abundantly now.

Thankfully, I give back to Him, at least ten percent of all I receive, and I get back a hundredfold! I am grateful!

I now let go, release completly, all false, negative, small, limiting thoughts, concepts and attitudes.

God-directed, I now move freely and easily into my unlimited success and prosperity.

Divine love fulfills my every good desire and I am rejoicing in my beautiful, happy, healthy and prosperous results now! I am grateful!

LOVE prospers me now in Health, Happiness, Joy, Peace, and Financial Plenty. Thank You, Father, I am grateful!

My goals are clear. My faith is strong. God within me makes me totally successful now. I am grateful!

I am prosperity! I now wisely give my energy to setting and achieving high goals.

I lift my vision and let God direct me in His ways of loving, wise, happy and prosperous living now.

I am grateful for rich abundance now!

I live in a rich, opulent universe of infinite plenty now.

I now claim and accept my rich good and pass it on to others.

My giving is making me richer and richer every day in every way now! I am grateful!

I dwell on thoughts of Plenty! Plenty!

The universe in which I live and which lives in me, is lavishly abundant with infinite good. I now claim and accept my fair share.

I love and bless all people with more and more of God's infinite riches.

I give thanks for everyone's rich prosperity now.

Infinite wisdom guides me, divine love prospers me, and I am successful in everything I undertake.

In quietness and confidence I affirm the drawing power of divine love as my magnet of ever-increasing rich supply.

I have unbounded faith in the omnipresent substance increasing and multiplying at my word of plenty, plenty, plenty.

I trust the universal Spirit of prosperity in all my affairs.

I give freely and fearlessly, fulfilling the law of giving and receiving.

Divine love, through me, blesses and multiplies all that I give.

Divine love, through me, blesses and multiplies all the money I receive, all the money I have, and all the money I give.

I have the FEELING of prosperity now!

Giving to Life what I want Life to give to me, I now quietly and confidently accept my abundant good.

Love lavishly prospers me now! I am grateful!

I set my goals by writing them down knowing definitely what I desire to achieve.

No matter what happens, I go serenely and confidently on my way.

With each challenge comes extra strength, ideas, courage, and everything necessary for my unlimited success and prosperity.

I give thanks for God's unfailing help as I persist. My success and prosperity are assured now. I am grateful!

Quietly, I relax away all worry, doubts and fears. I am free from all disturbing outside stimuli.

I picture my good and see it as mine now.

I am using my mind to create lavishly abundant prosperity and success for myself now.

I give thanks for my always increasing good health, happiness, harmony, and financial success now.

Freely and joyously, I share my rich good in blessing others. My giving comes back to me ten and a hundredfold now. I am grateful!

I now unlock and set free—my unlimited prosperity potential!

I now release all blocks to my prosperity. I am free of all that would keep me from my rich good now.

I now dare to free myself from all limiting thoughts, feelings and circumstances.

I totally release all resentment and unforgiveness of myself and others.

I take offense at nothing. I am free.

I am surging forward, divinely guided, into my new prosperous life now.

I boldly claim and accept my constantly increasing prosperity now.

I am prospering dynamically in beautiful, opulent ways now. I am grateful!

I speak my prospering word knowing divine substance is prospering myself and every person richly now.

I am a loving magnet for wealth and I now move forward, divinely guided, into my rich opulent good.

I am a mighty magnet for wealth! Elegant, palatial prosperity is irresistably drawn to me now.

I am a "Prosperity-Type" person. And, I act like it!

Every day in every way, I am growing in Prosperity Consciousness.

I see myself as prosperous now! I am!

All that I think, say, and do is Prosperous.

Thank You, Father-God, for all your rich good pouring into my life and affairs now.

I am grateful for your unlimited rich supply.

✿✿✿✿

Gratefully, I give my tenth to God, the source of all wealth, and my prosperity overflows in streams of lavish abundance now. I am grateful.

I now hasten my prosperity through tithing.

I freely give my tenth to God and he now gives to me a hundredfold.

Tithing faithfully, makes me permanently wealthy. This is so now. I am grateful!

My attitude of gratitude is my assurance of continued increasing financial abundance in my life now.

Tithing is my way of saying "Thank You, Father" for Your prospering substance always flowing abundantly into my life and affairs.

✿✿✿✿

I have LARGE, definite prosperity goals.

I now relax, let go and release old, worn-out concepts.

I now freely move on up to my rich good, divinely directed.

God is prospering me richly and abundantly now. I now dare to be rich!

I am moving forward in love, peace, freedom and rich abundance now. I am grateful!

I am an alive, active, enthusiastic and prospering member of the human race now!

I am grateful for the rich lavish abundance that keeps pouring into my life every day.

I am creating my prosperity first by making it a habit of thinking prosperously.

I am naturally "addicted" to prosperity now! I am grateful!

I now relax, let go, and release all that could possibly block my unlimited prosperity.

I am now free from worn-out thoughts and beliefs in lack and limitation.

I am cooperating fully with all spiritual laws and principles of prosperity now.

Freely and gratefully, I now accept God's infinite wealth as mine now. Thank You, Father. I am grateful!

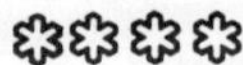

I now relax and use my alive and active imagination to clearly visualize and "experience" my goals as mine now.

My "Prosperity-Producing Mechanism" automatically brings prosperous results to me now.

I see and accept myself as a prosperous person now!

I love prosperity and prosperity loves me!

My success and prosperity are unlimited now! I am grateful!

My prosperous mental attitude produces marvelous abundance for me now!

I discipline myself to think only prosperous thoughts and I persist in my effort toward my prosperity goals, knowing that, right now, I am growing richer and richer. I give thanks for rich results now!

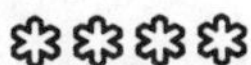

It is right to be rich. It is right for *me* to be rich. It is right for me to be exceedingly rich now!

I now dare to claim and accept my share of the unlimited riches of the universe.

I boldly step out in faith, BELIEVING, every day, in every way, I am growing richer and richer.

As the rich child of a loving Father, I now claim and accept my immediate increasing, and permanent prosperity.

Rich, prosperous results now manifest in God's own beautiful way for me and for all now! I am grateful!

I am free from the past and from all lack and limitation.

I now go forth into my new life of total prosperity.

I am financially wealthy, happy, loving, understanding, creative, and completely fulfilled now.

I am living graciously now, by the grace of God. I am grateful!

Divine Love is guiding, healing, harmonizing, and prospering me now! I am grateful!

I now relax, let go, and LOVE!

Divine Love is prospering me and everyone lavishly now!

The wisdom, love, and power of God are in absolute control of my life, creating perfect results here and now!

My mind is open to the miracle of prospering ideas.

God in me, is my unlimited Source of wealth.

Divinely guided, I now give, give, and give, and I enjoy plenty! plenty! plenty!

I am expecting "unexpected income!" All avenues are open to me now.

Turning within to my unlimited Cosmic Power, I tap this rich reservoir of wealth and success for happy, prosperous living.

Giving freely and joyously, I receive in the same way. The more I give, the more I receive. I cannot outgive God!

God in me is my assurance of success.

Turning within, I ask for divine guidance, I listen and follow through on that guidance.

With God guiding me all the way, I am successful in all that I undertake.

I know what to do and I do it. My prosperity is growing by leaps and bounds now. I am grateful!

All channels are free! All doors are open!

God is my help in every need. He is within me as my never-failing supply.

I now accept, in faith, believing—my rich, ever-increasing prosperity.

Since giving is the first part of receiving, I give freely and receive abundantly now.

All that is mine by divine right is now released and reaches me in great avalanches of abundance, under grace in marvelous ways now!

Thank You, Father-God, for overflowing, beautiful prosperity now!

Christ in me, is my source of rich ideas.

Seeking within, I am now guided in ways of success and prosperity.

New, prospering ideas are now revealed and prosper me richly and abundantly now.

God in me, is my Guide and my rich supply.

He is guiding me in ways of true happiness, peace and prosperity now.

My mind is open, my heart is receptive, and miracles are happening to me now!

I give thanks for avalanches of rich prosperity blessings now.

I now release the gold mine within me. I am united with an endless golden stream of rich prosperity which comes to me under grace in perfect ways now.

There are no obstacles in Divine Mind, therefore, there is nothing to obstruct my rich good.

All obstacles now vanish from my pathway. Doors open wide, gates are lifted and I enjoy rich, lavish fulfillment now!

My mind is open and my heart is receptive to God's vast rich good for me now.

I have released all old, small, worn-out concepts and beliefs about my prosperity.

I give thanks for visible prosperity overflowing in my life now.

My mind is open and I am receptive to the vast riches of the universe now.

Riches are my divine right. Every day, in every way, I am becoming more and more prosperous in God's good way.

I am surrounded by substance, which is always taking the form of rich, unlimited supply and always manifesting itself for me in the form of whatever my need may be at the time.

I give thanks for the abundance of God expressed in my personal affairs now.

I have an abundance to spare and to share, today and forever. And, I DO share it, now.

I give that I may receive: Nor do I wait until I receive before I give.

The Law of rich supply works beautifully in my affairs because I keep my supply in beautiful circulation now.

❁❁❁❁

Love is prospering energy. Everything I do is done in love.

I think love. I give love. I radiate love to everything and every person.

Love comes back to me in avalanches of rich, beautiful prosperity now. I am grateful!

LOVE—The Resurrecting Power of Jesus Christ, is mightily at work in my mind, body, life and affairs now.

Love is what I am. I am now being what I am: LOVE!

✿✿✿✿

Knowing that God is all-powerful and that I am one with His power, I build an attitude for successful living.

I turn from thoughts of inadequacy and formulate ideas of effective achievement.

New and greater areas of creative expression are now open to me and I move forward and upward to higher levels of successful accomplishment now.

God-ideas permeate my mind and affairs with success, and I am lavishly prospered in every good way now. I am grateful!

The millions that are divinely and rightly mine, pour in and heap up in copious mountains of riches under grace in marvelous ways for me now.

Money now comes to me from every direction because I am an irresistable magnet of Divine Love now.

Divine order is now established in my financial affairs. Divine order now establishes me in overflowing, luxurious, financial freedom now.

Faithfully, consistently and lovingly giving my ten percent to God, provides me with avalanches of rich, magnificent financial abundance now.

Tithing has freed me from all struggle and striving. I gratefully give my tenth and now I'm thriving!

The Wisdom, Love, and Power of God are in absolute control of my life, creating perfect results, here and now!

It is my Father's good pleasure to give me His treasure in marvelous measure, now!

God works in unexpected and magic ways His wonders to perform. I now prepare for the fulfillment of my heart's desires.

✽✽✽✽

Daily I build my prosperity consciousness by using prosperous words.

I am open and receptive to prospering ideas and alert to use them.

Christ in me is my prospering power. I am richly prospered in all my ways now.

My prosperity consciousness now produces immediate rich supply in great avalanches of abundance.

I now dare to grow!

I am now open to new ideas and challenges for growth and success.

With God's help, I have all I need to be extremely successful and lavishly prospered now.

I am successful and prosperous now, and I am grateful.

Thank You, Father, for my unlimited potential.

Seeking within myself I ask for, expect, and accept rich ideas. I am open and receptive now.

Divinely guided, I do all I can to help make my dreams come true.

❃❃❃❃

As in ancient times, TEN is still the magic number of increase.

Faithfully giving my tenth to God assures me of financial freedom and plenty.

Freely tithing at least ten percent of my gross income assures my success.

As a consistent tither, my affairs are in divine order, I am divinely protected, and there is always plenty to spare and to share.

I now tithe my way to success and prosperity.

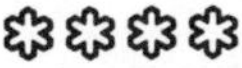

Christ in me is my healing power now.

Christ in me is my prospering power now.

Christ in me is my overcoming power now.

The resurrecting power of Jesus Christ lifts me into new life, love, and prosperous living now.

Thank You, God, for my ever-increasing awareness of your Infinite Presence in my mind, body and affairs now.

Seeming impossible doors are open, seeming impossible channels are free, in the name of Jesus Christ.

I now claim and accept my rich heritage of happiness, health, prosperity, and freedom, here and now.

God's very best, opulent lavish good is now pouring copiously into my life and affairs and I am living in grand and gracious style with ease now.

I am grateful!

✿✿✿✿✿✿✿✿✿✿✿✿✿✿✿✿✿✿✿✿✿✿✿✿✿✿✿✿

Thank You, God, for
Answered Prayer
I know Your Good
is everywhere.

I'm open, receptive,
and I believe
Vast good is mine,
and I now receive!

Listening within,

God shows the way

And I am prospered

more each day!

God is giving,
and I'm believing . . .
All His riches,
I'm now receiving.

My mind is open,
my hands are, too . . .
God is blessing me
richly in all I do!

All doors to my good

are open and free;

And

God is now giving

His best to me!

It is my Father's

good pleasure

to give me His treasure

in marvelous measure!

Now!

God's rich supply

is on its way—

In Love, I gratefully

accept mine today!

We know that
God will never cease
To give us all,
His Love and Peace.

God within is
our rich supply—
He's always giving to
You and I!

God Bless You!

God's infinite good now blesses every phase of your life. His Love fills your heart making you an irresistible magnet for happy experiences, warm and true friends, and lavish financial abundance. His Life permeates your mind and body making you strong, healthy, and perfect. God in you, gives you peace and joy making your life beautiful, joyous, positive, prosperous, and exciting now! God bless you, my friend. You deserve the very best! This book will help you have it!

A personal note

I love you. I want you to experience prosperous living in the very highest way. My prayer is that this book is of real help to you in doing that. If you care to write, I will be happy to hear of how this book is helping you to live the prosperous life.

John Wolcott Adams
P.O. Box 1463
Mesa, AZ 85211-1463 USA